I THINK I THOUGHT

I THINK I THOUGHT

Martin Parker

Matador
9 Priory Business Park,
Wistow Road, Kibworth Beauchamp,
Leicestershire. LE8 0RX
Tel: 0116 279 2299
Email: books@troubador.co.uk
Web: www.troubador.co.uk/matador
Twitter: @matadorbooks

ISBN 9781788037556

British Library Cataloguing in Publication Data.
A catalogue record for this book is available from the British Library.

Printed by TJ International, Padstow, Cornwall, UK
Typeset in 11pt Aldine by Troubador Publishing Ltd, Leicester, UK

Matador is an imprint of Troubador Publishing Ltd

Several of these pieces, or earlier versions of them, first appeared in a variety of publications including *The Spectator, The Literary Review* and *The Oldie* as well as in web-zines including *Lighten Up Online* and *Light*. Some can be found in *No Longer Bjored*, published in 2010 by Happen*Stance*.

CONTENTS

About Getting Better At It   45

The View From Codgers Corner   63

About Getting Near the Buffers   91

About Getting Started

Joining a family – living with it, surviving it and managing to grow up despite it.

Then starting your own and soon wondering whether any of them can be even distantly related to you.

Day Two

Already I've grown really tired
of being constantly admired
by all these strangers who now come
to cluck and coo and pat my bum,
who say I've stolen someone's nose
then fiddle with my hands and toes,
who can't tell smiles from painful wind,
or that I'd rather drink milk tinned.

There's nothing here to make me happy –
and all Hell festers in my nappy.

Baby Brother

My baby brother's ten days old.
The smell of nappies turns me cold.

Mum thinks he smells of milk and soap.
All babies do, she says. Some hope!

He's not as sweet as my Mum thinks.
He's loud and wrinkled. And he stinks.

Since he was born I've learned to tell
Love's blind and deaf – and cannot smell.

Big Sister

When I was one
My sister was fun.

At two and three
She played with me.

But now I'm four
She locks her door

And tells me to get lost.

Same Sister, But Bigger

At holiday time when boys are about
my sister takes hours getting dressed to go out
in very short skirts and very strong smells
designed to encourage wedding bells.

I wonder how it can take so long
to put on so little and be so wrong.

Granny

My Granny has a bristly chin.

I hope that she won't kiss me.

But if she tries I'll move my head

And hope her kiss will miss me.

.... and Don't Do That!

Don't listen at your sister's door
or ask her what her bra is for.
Don't drown your brother's Teddy Bear.
Don't tell your Dad he's lost more hair.
Don't bang in nails with his new bat.
And, till you're older, don't do THAT!

Don't count the hairs on Granny's chin
or tell her where we keep the gin.
Don't play with what was up your nose.
Don't cheer when Auntie Pauline goes.
Don't tease the dog or chase the cat.
And ABSOLUTELY DON'T DO THAT!

Wet Kiss

We met beside The Serpentine.
You kissed me in the rain,

Your Nanny saw you do it,
so we never met again.

The sound of rain on water
still keeps that kiss alive –
which is pretty bloody tragic
now I'm sixty-five.

Jill Battersby

Wet leaves lie deep along Wellington Avenue.
Bonfire smoke hangs in each skeleton tree.
Me with Jill Battersby, laughing and sliding,
Racing the dusk home for Nursery tea.

Cornering fast into Waterloo Crescent
I trip on a kerbstone and graze a bare knee,
A wound soon repaired by her lick on a hankie
And promise of honey and crumpets for tea.

Though seventy autumns have withered behind me
I still feel the thrill in the child that was me
At the little pink hearts round the edge of her hankie,
The smell of wet leaves and her taste on my knee.

New Shoes for Radioactive Feet

New shoes for school, at least four pairs a year
of stout black lace-ups; and extremely dear
at seventeen-and-six, my mother thought,
for feet which grew much faster than feet ought.
Shoes bought so large they scarcely touched in places
no matter quite how hard she tugged the laces
and packed each gap uncomfortably full
with insoles, thicker socks and cotton wool.

At last, to prove my point, we'd peer at those
small, wriggling skeletons inside my toes
beneath us on the green, fluorescent screen
of Harrod's X-ray "Check Your Fit" machine –
which left my mother with the false but firm
belief the shoes would last me one whole Term.

Early Learning

Rhona offered kisses for a penny,
Julie's playground currency was Mars.
Yana wanted Smarties, though not many,
Gina puckered up for Crunchie Bars.
Beth could be persuaded by a Rolo,
Izzie offered tongues for Custard Creams,
Vicky reached your tonsils for a Polo,
Martha, offered fudge, could fuel strange dreams.

Inflation set in at our Comp, Saint Barty's.
By sixteen little Yana had turned hard.
Gone the days when she'd accept three Smarties.
Yana soon required a Credit Card –
    Of which, for spotty schoolboys down in Hackney,
    Frequent applications cured our acne.

Prayer Before School Dinner

I am not yet fed; O hear me.
Let not the food police, diet freaks, killjoys or hectoring health cranks
    come anywhere near me.

I am not yet fed; provide me
with twizzlers to twizzle me, nuggets and burgers to nugget and
    burger me, sausage and chips and big second helpings
        of E-numbers, sugar and poly-unsaturates
            bound to account for me.

I am not yet fed; preserve me
from all healthy options and food with no fat in it,
    from fruit juice and salad and yoghurt and tofu,
        from mean, thin-crust pizza and fish that's been steamed,
            and from all types of vegetables.

I am not yet fed; help me
    to bunk off from dinner and find my way home
        via McDonald's and Burger King, sweet-shops and fizzy drinks;
            then to miss Games and all forms of exercise
                each day this week.

And I will not care so long as meals fill me.
    Although they may kill me.

Valentine

I bought you red roses, a big box of chocs
and a gross red plush card with a heart that unlocks.

But the heat of the words in the heart that unlocks
withered the roses and melted the chocs.

So all I have left is dead stalks and a box
and this gross red plush card with the heart that unlocks.

Is there still a chance you might agree to come out with me?

Teenage Party

Somewhere under this pile of coats
is the girl I nearly made love with,
the girl who, only ten minutes ago,
I was under, beside and above with;
the girl who made a meal of me
then threw up on the floor;
the one who went to use the loo
but couldn't find the door;
the one who, now the light is on,
looks at least twenty years old;
the one who said some unflattering things
before she passed out cold.

I'd hate to wake her up again
but Mum is expecting me back.
Besides, I think it's started to rain.
So I need to find my mac.

Living Next Door To Emily

She said that I was just a kid
and that I shouldn't;
that she'd been warned against it
and therefore wouldn't.

At last, when I was not a kid,
she did.
And I was so amazed
I almost couldn't.

Mutants From The Planet Zog

So, *amor vincit omnia*, they say?
Well, not for every parent every day.

An alien force now rules your life.
Not again! you tell your wife.

And, though you both agree, it's still
more than likely that you will.

For Man is weak. Love's urge is stronger.
Tumescence brevis, penance longer.

Cuckoo In The Nest

I've stuffed my one chick on a diet of worm
and the sorts of small insects that robins like best.
But now it's the size of a small pachyderm
and its wings hang far over both sides of my nest.
And it's far from becoming a robin.

Its colouring, too, makes me ask myself whether
my efforts are wasted. For each day I think
that there's less and less prospect that even one feather
is turning bright red yet – or even pale pink–
to suggest it's becoming a robin.

I've ruptured my larynx to teach it to chirp
in a twittering, chirruping, robinish trill.
But all I've got back is an ill-sounding "Burp."
Still, I live with the hope that tomorrow it will
say "Cheep" and behave like a robin.

It's a thankless great heap. It's the size of a Jeep.
Its feathers aren't red and its voice is too deep.
They say as you sow then that's how you shall reap,
and I've sown weeks of love on this graceless young creep.
But I fear it requires more than one massive leap
of faith to believe it's a robin.

Elegy Written On A Cornish Beach

EastEnders tolls the knell of parting day,
the shrimp-pink grockles wobble from the sea.
The call of fish and chips now clears the bay
and leaves the scene to litter and to me.

Here pokes my head from out a mound of sand
a father by his family interred;
their grizzled patriarch and guiding hand
abandoned by his homeward rushing herd.

A moment's gentle sleep was all I'd sought,
brief respite from the hunter-gatherer's lot
before the evening's cod and chips were bought.
Forgotten in the rush was what I got.

No more will I extol as once I did
the loyalties and joys of family life.
A nest of vipers lurks beneath the lid
of seaside holidays with kids and stressed-out wife.

Janet And John

Well spoken, well mannered, with well scrubbed bare knees,
eager to listen, to learn, help and please,
politely correct but politically non –
John with his Janet and Janet with John.

Shining examples of fine English youth,
models of loyalty, honour and truth –
middle-class values now sadly long gone
down History's plughole with Janet and John.

It is hard to accept that our children have grown,
that those we once read to have kids of their own;
while the children we wished for them only belong
in our dog-eared old pages of Janet and John.

Going for Broke

When you've grown far too old to be useful,
when your family all think you're a bore,
say "Nuts" to the lot of them;
simply get shot of them.
That's what world cruises are for.

So tear up your Will. Book a State-room.
Though the thought of a cruise may appal,
set sail for the best state
of dead and intestate
with assets of nothing at all.

You can't spend your cash when you've snuffed it.
Your kids think they should. But so what?
Go sit in the Diner
of some plushy liner
and spend till you've got through the lot.

About Getting It Wrong, Mostly

Hope, love and commonsense spring less than eternal.

Signal Failure

I'm bewildered, as men often can be,
knowing even when things get intense
that women give out such mixed signals
men can't tell *Come Hither* from *Hence*!

But a man's body language is simple
and our small print is easy to read.
We're not subtle. It's plain as a pikestaff
when it's more than a smile that we need.

But with women it's all down to guesswork.
Though they may imply Yes, all men know
that it's hard to tell two seconds later
whether what seemed a *Yes* is now *No*.

So I'm standing here anxious and puzzled
as the signs of my ardour increase.
If I summon the courage to kiss you
will you let me – or call the Police?

Please!

Wagging, panting and eager
each day I bring you sticks.

All that you do
is throw them away.

But I bring them back,
still panting and hoping

that one day you'll realise
they are for you.

Travelling In Hope

You were nervous in Nantes and Nancy
And virginal in the Vosges.
In Bucharest you were too depressed
And suddenly shy in Limoges.
You were queasy in Tibilisi
And timid in far Tashkent.
In Samarkand you held my hand;
But that was as far as you went.

You relaxed the ban one night in Cannes:
Though I'm very much afraid
That after a second you clearly reckoned
My welcome had been outstayed.

And then back home in England
You were lustless in Leamington Spa,
Frigid in Frinton and Aston Clinton
And non-priapic in Par.
So till you make your mind up
Whether sex is right for you
I'm off to Alice in Crystal Palace
Or laid-back Lucy in Looe.

Woo Her With Wine

Woo her with wine
and diamonds and laughter,
then make the best
of all that comes after.

Suffer her tantrums,
soothe all her ills;
say she's still slim
and pay all the bills.

Don't dwell on her errors –
well, not for too long.
But sometimes believe
that *you* might be wrong.

And tell her that yours
is a love like no other –
even when she
has turned into her mother.

Triolet For A Misspent Weekend

My weekend was spent on wine, women and song.
I knew it was wrong; but it felt oh so right.
I tried to resist but their call was too strong.
My weekend was spent on wine, women and song.

My only regret was it didn't take long
to render me knackered, sore-throated and tight.
My weekend was spent on wine, women and song.
I knew it was wrong; but it felt oh so right!

A Book At Bedtime

With your constant "splitting head"
How come you read so much in bed?

Or is it just to hide your stress
At waiting till I detumesce?

Giving Up

For you I gave up beer and pubs,
two-seater cars, exotic clubs,
fluorescent condoms, one night stands,
a credit balance and rock bands,
my flat, Black Book and social life,
most of my bed and someone else's wife.

And you? You gave up sex for both of us
and called me selfish when I made a fuss.

Private Viewing

Porn has an under-rated use.
It tires men out with self-abuse.

For wives who view sex with a frown
This serves to keep a good man down.

Chucking-out Time

I threw myself at you and, in return,
you've thrown back glasses, plates, an antique urn,
the fragile shrapnel of our war-torn life,
a clock, fish pie, a garden gnome, a knife,
soap, doughnuts and a plate of greasy mince,
hot coffee, saucepans and my hunting prints,
the soaking contents of a kitchen sink,
a shelf of books, your muesli, make-up, ink,
a garden fork, the car keys and a jack ......

I threw myself at you. Please, throw me back.

Moving

This house has been wrecked by our marriage;
Its fabric now flakes with each fight.
Its fixtures and fittings all hate us.
They think we should move – and they're right.

The loo seat is icy with anger,
The doorbell is dumb with disgust,
Resentment's corroded the plumbing,
The heating's been chilled by mistrust.
The front door has slammed off its hinges,
The taps are jammed tight as a truss.
The freezer runs hot on pure hatred.
This house now regrets that we're us.

But habit still keeps us together
And inertia makes very strong glue.
So the house has decided to move on its own
And leave us together to stew.

After You

Now that you've gone and my life has moved on
and I'm done with the hum and the drum of you
and your multiple lies and my lack of surprise
at the dust of the crust and the crumb of you …

plus the times you returned despite bridges you'd burned
and the mad and the bad and the sad of you
and the woes and the pose and the lowest of lows
and the near-total absence of glad of you …

and the yeses, the noes and the stops and the goes
and the what and the not and the blot of you
and the hows and the rows and the who's-to-blame-nows
I am truly relieved that I'm shot of you.

Now my life is much better, each day more red letter,
though there's something I can't quite explain about
my regret that I mind when I wake up and find
that you're no longer here to complain about.

When I Owned Number Twenty

When I owned Number Twenty
    I heard a wise man say,
"Give crowns and pounds and guineas
    But not your house away.
Give pearls away and rubies
    But keep your freehold free."
But I was young and much in love.
    No use to talk to me.

When she moved into Twenty
    I heard him say again,
"Joint occupancy of one's house
    Will some day bring you pain.
The Law will give her plenty
    And there's nothing you can do."
Now she's got Number Twenty
    And the weekend cottage too.

Spare Man

I'm reliably sober and charming,
I'm single, well-mannered and free.
So when hostesses, planning a dinner,
need one more man they ask me.

I've spent hours being kind to the silent,
the tragic, the lonely, the plain,
the divorced, the deserted, the dreary
and those for whom men are a pain.

I've been groped by the recently widowed
and also – it's par for the course –
I've been leered at by large ugly ducklings
with molars too big for a horse.

I've suffered while feminist poets
have bored me with slabs of their verse.
I've had syphilis spelled out in detail
by a graphic young STD Nurse.

I've been sought as a suitor by Sirens
who've had far more partners than wheels
on all Eddie Stobart's big lorries,
or quacks in a duck, or hot meals.

(cont.)

But I never let on that I'm lonely,
though sometimes I know I can see,
as we swap our dull, desperate small-talk,
a sad mirror image of me.

For, in truth, I'm as eager as they are
to achieve a relationship, please,
that will last just a little bit longer
than the time between starter and cheese.

A Prayer Regarding Unsuitable Women

Lord, in your charity, let me forget
the many unsuitable women I've met.

Clear my mind of them, and yet
please make sure *they* don't forget.

And grant me a chance to recoup the cost
of those I foolishly loved and lost.

In the name of the Father and the Son
who lent me several just for fun.

Down And Out Behind A Desk

The generation that survived two Wars and The Depression
passed down to me their soul-destroying, deep-ingrained impression
that life required allegiance to that middle-class convention,
a job with real security, good prospects and a pension.

No matter just how dead-end dull were Banking and Insurance
their safe respectability held out the reassurance
of solid British worthiness and values, rather than
of unrelenting 9 to 5 futility for Man.

And so I joined a City firm in which I had the loan
of tea-stained desk, a swivel chair and greasy telephone
for forty years of apathy that saw the end of dreams
and dimmed the hope that life might be less humdrum than it seems.

Not long from now I'll get my clock and farewell glass of wine
while one more fool will quietly fill the chair that has been mine.
And then perhaps I'll have the chance to find what life's about
before the random sands of time can count me down and out.

Rat Race

The corporate radials stop and soon grow cold
as one more peak-hour traffic jam, foretold
to last from Junction One to Twenty-three,
brings every lane of traffic to its knees.

And middle management is held becalmed,
ambition and achievement all embalmed
in each tin box held fast in time and space
like freeze-framed runners in a frozen race

while ulcered underlings in anxious state
all curse and sweat and hyperventilate
at meetings unattended, targets missed,
at deadlines passed and PAs left un-kissed.

For these sad souls the Universe has stopped.
And nails are chewed, teeth ground and foreheads mopped
awaiting just the clearing of one lane
to let the wheels of Life turn once again.

Fantasy Theme Bars

We tried our shy machismo on the red-lipped women
round at "Hemingway's",
measured out our youth with coffee spoons and poetry
down at "Eliot's"
and waited for enlightenment at "Beckett's".

Now redevelopment has moved the women on
from Hemingway's,
called Last Orders on the scalding cappuccino
down at Eliot's
and spewed a by-pass on the beer-bedraggled floor
of Beckett's.

Now, each suburban Sunday in the Wetherspoon's
we once called "Kerouac's"
we meet to talk, for just one cautious pint, of children,
mortgages and lawn sand;
then leave to walk the dogs, to look at colour charts
and cut the grass.

And I am mocked by all the ghosts from Hemingway's,
still hoping for the poetry I almost wrote at Eliot's,
still waiting for the myth that never quite arrived at Beckett's:
a stranger in the memory of places that we'd named
to house our dreams.

Life On Mars

My Mum had read the diet books and planned my mealtimes properly.
She fed me lots of healthy stuff like wholemeal bread and broccoli.
But after school each afternoon I sat in chippie bars
and gorged on Glasgow's favourite snack of deep-fried battered Mars.

At ten I had cherubic looks. By thirteen what I'd got
were cheeks just like a pizza top with every pore a spot
of suppurating acne which exploded like Mount Etna
and was visible in Glasgow from as far away as Gretna.

I've been obese for fifty years. Of strokes I've had a hat-trick.
My bedroom floor is reinforced, my bed is bariatric.
I stand (though standing's difficult) to warn against indulgence
in comfort food that's full of saturated fat's effulgence.

The Undertaker tells me that he doubts there is a coffin
that's big enough and strong enough for him to take me off in
and warns me that he fears my final journey to the stars
is likely to be hindered by my lifetime spent on Mars.

Tattooed Brenda

When, plagued by commonsense and rational thought,
I contemplate the weight of rancid grease
I have consumed in years of breakfasts bought
In Tattooed Brenda's Caff I never cease
To sense the kiss of death in every plate
Of saturated-fat-fried egg and chips
And all those bits, well past their sell-by date,
Of sausage made from sphincters, ears and lips.

And though her greeting call may sound alarms –
Oh, God! It's you again! today's selection –
The 'LOVE' 'HATE' knuckles on her black-inked arms
Suggest perhaps a half chance of affection.
So, though I know her food is to abhor,
May God tomorrow grant me one plate more;
For nothing else can make a day seem rosier
Than Tattooed Brenda's greasy fried ambrosia.

School Reunion "Nite"

Like me they'd had dandruff and terrible spots
                 and that lurking testosterone smell
which pervaded the bike-sheds at Hackney Sec. Mod.
                 As a group we had failed to excel
at anything much except dreaming of sex;
                 for most of each term-time had been
spent staring up Jennifer Jenkinson's skirt
                 and dreaming of what we'd not seen.

But Friday's Reunion "Nite" at The Grand
                 convinced me, for what it is worth,
that it isn't the meek but the mentally bleak
                 who have come to inherit the earth.
Viz., Alastair Lloyd, of grey matter devoid,
                 with his E Grade in Media Studies
has been Head of TV and of Radio 3
                 and is one of the D G's best buddies.

The rest are all rock stars, celebrity cooks,
                 Big Brother contestants – or worse,
for Anthony Frame who could scarce spell his name
                 has published two books of light verse...
While middle-aged me, with two As and a B,
                 having married a girl who's now Kurt,
am pockmarked from acne, still living in Hackney,
                 still dreaming of Jennifer's skirt.

Click On Delete

I was less than delighted
                    with Friends Reunited,

for the friends I'd once had
                    were still just as bad.

About Getting The Hang Of It

...of age – of each other – of life – of the past and the future –
of love and gentler laughter.

The Rover's Return

Jane was young and so was Kitty.
Love with them rang briefly true.
Kate was kind and Jill was pretty.
But always I came home to you.

Sally's hands brought gentle healing,
Jenny's eyes were baby blue,
Jo's lips soft, Nell's smile appealing.
Love was all that Mary knew.

And now I'm old and dreams are over
I bring you roses sprigged with rue
And beg you to forgive this rover
Who makes his last way home to you.

Climate Change

When I was young
July was hot –

    Now it's not.

When I was young
I was hot –

    Now I'm not.

July and I
Have gone badly awry.

    Why, when you've not?

At Home

For risking five quick minutes unexpected love
between the summer border and the raspberry canes,
you still in wellies and one gardening glove,
we find ourselves, a cartographical mishap,
spreadeagled pink and only slightly blurred,
"At Home" to all the world upon a Googlemap.

Not Quite James Dean

You're not the girl I dreamed of in my youth,
Brigitte Bardot seal-sleek from the shower,
kisses laced with wine and passion fruit.

But I'm not quite the man I dreamed I was.

Thank you for not reminding me of that
across our prim-pyjama'd cocoa
and the Daily Telegraph.

In The Attic

You cleared the attic space of bags of clothes
from days pre-stretch-marks, lines and cellulite
and sat sad-eyed among them on our bed.
I shan't be needing these again, you said.
I've reached the age when even Large is tight.

Then love surprised us on your mothballed past
of miniskirts, the Lurex tops that shone,
the Demis Roussos kaftan like a tent,
those hot-pants and the tights for which you'd bent
your hips into contortions pulling on.

And afterwards we lay there on the heap
still crackling from its Sixties nylon static:
and, though the Size 8 girl I'd loved had gone,
the new one still felt good with nothing on
and two thirds of her time stored in our attic.

Box And Cox

We'd settled successfully into our rut
where sex is no more than a memory. But
along came this wunderkind boffin Brian Cox
for whom my wife waits open-mouthed by our Box.
And though, to my mind, he's distinctly androgynous
he reaches her parts that she once found erogenous.
I've tried to persuade her that frisky is risky,
that what once stood tall is now less obelisky:
and were we to try something so cataclysmic,
I doubt we could now re-create paroxysmic,
and Bangs, Big or Small, in Acacia Villas
as likely as not would exhaust if not kill us.
    So please, for the sake of our welfare, Brian Cox,
    Keep your brain to yourself and your face off our Box.

Twenty-One Again

You walk into the room
and long-dead dreams all come alive;
and I am twenty-one again
at sixty-five.

And I can see, each time your smile
and laughter lead me on,
that I was all too often sixty-five
at twenty-one.

Come Jive With Me

Come jive with me and be my love
And with a glitter-ball above
Let's join the dance-floor's push and shove
And re-create our Sixties love.

The jive of our frenetic youth
Is too demanding now. In truth
The jive may not be quite the dance
For pensioners who'd fan romance.

Our knees and backs won't stand the strain
And violent movement causes pain.
Too soon we'll find a loss of puff'll
Mock our geriatric shuffle.

But, what the Hell! We're still alive
And love's still blind at sixty-five.
So, till we're eighty or above
Come jive with me – but slowly, love.

Yours Sincerely, Wasting Away

Hearing '60's music makes me sad,

because

it now reminds me just how long ago

I was.

Tilting the Balance

You stood, eyes shut, upon the scales
you'd begged me hide.
You said, "I must be thirteen stone
with this backside."
And I, who'd loved you
since your slim-line youth,
opted for discretion, not the truth;
and made a liar of your scales and me.
"Not you," I said. "You're almost down
to twelve stone three."

About Face

For huge sums of money
    you had your face lifted.
But since it was done
    it's clear some bits have shifted.

Though your cheeks are less wrinkled
    and chins far less slack
you are harder to kiss
    now your mouth's round the back.

Little Black Dress

She looked two sizes smaller in her little wisp of black.
She sparkled on the dance-floor and then she asked him back.

And firelight, lace and brandy made her confident he saw
the size the dress had made her feel before it hit the floor.

To The Saturday Girl In The Newspaper Shop

Thank you for not chewing gum or saying, "Yeah,"
    or painting all your fingernails bright green;

for never wearing tongue studs, lace designer-mittens
    or tee-shirts sniggering with double meaning;

for smiling cheerfully at someone old enough
    to interest no-one but undertakers;

for always moving The Spectator from the Sports shelf
    and having read my poem there today;

for telling me your plans for university
    and for your next week's brave new hair colour;

for asking my advice about what car to buy
    and never having spoken of a boyfriend;

and making me remember seventeen again
    as though I had been sharing it with you.

Marriage Vows To A Daughter

We promise not to disapprove
     if you should break the patterns which we set,
     vote Green, pay most bills late and not eat fruit,
     spend Christmas not with us, and out of touch.
We promise not to disapprove –
     well, not too much.

We promise not to criticise
     your husband, housework, china, choice of friends,
     your worst decisions, how you spend your cash,
     your car, your lifestyle, furniture and such.
We promise not to criticise –
     well, not too much.

We promise not to nag and fuss
     and phone to ask if you've sent Gran a card,
     or how much longer we must store your stuff,
     or say we're hurt you haven't been in touch.
We promise not to nag and fuss –
     well, not too much.

We promise to respect your space,
     the fact that you've moved on and have a life
     where we are visitors though, maybe still,
     if drowning's near, a straw that's there to clutch.
We promise still to love, though from a distance –
     but just as much.

A Cinquain For Emily

I know
that when I'm old
I'll still remember you
long after I've stopped groping for
your name.

Remember Me

Remember me if I should go awry
and can't remember who or how or why
either of us is or used to be
when I was me and you and I were we.

Remember me if I should go awry.
But if, like me, you can't – at least please try.

The View from Codgers Corner

Nothing is as good as it used to be in your day – and people are less willing than they should be to listen to you talking about it.

Eeyore At Christmas

A Pox on the Christmas Spirit,
and Humbug to Seasonal Cheer
which lasts for a week in December
and dies with the bells of New Year.

Then pine needles clog up the Hoover
and problems pile up by the yard.
Good Wishes are too often transient things,
whatever it said on the card.

New Gods For Old

A Planning Notice on our churchyard gate
Proclaims the end of God in Brambley Down,
His plot now destined for a tarmacked fate
As link-road for the motorway to town.

Soon men will come to move these lichened stones
And then in high-viz jackets dig our dead
To sacrifice the sanctity of bones
For faster trips to Sainsbury's instead.

Then will our hallowed spot have sunk to this –
From golden gateway for celestial souls,
To quicker access to terrestrial bliss
Via tins of Beanz and BOGOF toilet rolls.

Sepia Giants

My grandad took that photograph. Eleven village men,
his proudly staring sepia team of Summer nineteen-ten,
who lived as custom ordered them and touched their caps to Squire;
who dug his ditches, worked his fields and died in Flanders mire.
Eleven faded summer men caught by camera flash
now, curled on the pavilion wall, still cut their nameless dash.

But who will find our present team so honourable a place?
week-enders who have bought us cheap and scrubbed our rural face
and torn up cottage gardens, laying concrete to their doors,
for easy space in which to park their City 4 x 4s;
whose rural idyll jangles with alarms and double locks;
who've priced our village children into distant tower blocks;

while each drives off when stumps are drawn to sit beside his pool
at The Old Almshouse, Old Bakery, Old Stables and Old School,
past the names of Grandad's giants on a tall cross in the Square
while the sepia ghosts of nineteen-ten, uncomprehending, stare.

No Entry

They shut the road through the woods
When the Planning Authority said
That what was really needed
Was a Motorway instead.

A country lane, the Council said,
Was about as little use
As a chocolate teapot, a DPM
Or marshmallow horns on a moose.

Then Health and Safety decided
That woods are dangerous things
And imposed the daft restrictions
That Health and Safety brings.

So, having built the Motorway
The Council Straight From Hell
Not only shut the woodland road
But shut the woods as well.

Caught Short

I had a penny,
A bright new penny.
I took my penny
   To the market square.
I needed a toilet,
A public toilet;
And I looked for a toilet
   'Most everywhere.

I had a problem,
An urgent problem,
A desperate problem
   With the market square.
For the public toilet
Was now a gift shop.
So I wet my Y-fronts
   In the market square.

The Wind Farm Of Shalott

Last week The Green Brigade came by
And clothed the wold and met the sky
With whirling monoliths on high
From here to Camelot.

Now all day long within my room
I'll hear their constant swish and boom
Until the very Crack of Doom
Supplying Camelot.

Where every cup of tea they make
And every bath and shower they take
Reminds me just how much I hate
The Greens in Camelot.

Innhospitality

With Gallic guile new gastro-pubs now battle to excite us
with cuisine which they claim is "haute". Who wants haute enteritis?

They think to fool our palates now. But folk like you and I
know "pommes frites" do not real chips make nor "tarte tatin" a
pie.

Now qu'est-ce que c'est this thing "timbale" and what's a man to do
avec les caulifleurs du mal smeared on to plates as "jus"?

And take my tip, charcuterie's best eaten late at night.
It's cuts of meat you wouldn't want to look at in the light.

There's no amount of menu-French can cover up what's true –
these pubs are their revenge on us for winning Waterloo.

Invasion by more subtle means is what they're aiming at.
We'll fight them in The Crown, Queen's Arms, King's Head and
Cheshire Cat

so England's Public Houses can last a thousand years
as shrines of five star excellence to pies and luke-warm beers

instead of just surrendering to fussy French cuisine
whose garlic breath and Gallic bile once powered their guillotine.

(cont.)

Let's put an end to gastro-lies that French cuisine is tasty.
There's just one way to serve up food – and that's inside thick pastry,

that sign of reassurance for those not keen to grapple
with any cuisine "hauter" than chunks of meat or apple,

our English armour-plating wrapped round food you can be sure of;
the sort of plain, no-nonsense stuff all pubs should serve us more
of…

Où sont les beige meat pies d'antan inside my pub, The Star?
Dieu, que le nom du gastro-pub est triste au fond du bar!

In Praise Of Spam

Though gastronomes may sneer and titter
I'm proud to hymn the humble fritter
filled with pinkly blushing Spam,
related – so they swore – to ham;
limp obsolescence on a plate
exuding grease in oily spate,
the modern chefs' reviled outcast
memento of our rationed past.

But with Spam fritters what one got
was honest English food and not
today's weird mix of streaks and smears
which stir my taste-buds' darkest fears
that what we're being asked to eat
are crusted skid-marks as a treat.
God bless you, frittered Spam, for looking
just like proper English cooking.

from The Epic Of Sir Greasy Spoon

When Gastro-Pub The Ghastly
With henchmen Foam and Jus
Had poured foul scorn o'er all the best
Old England's cooks could do
One valiant knight swore solemnly
That 'ere the next full moon
He'd cook the vile intruder's goose –
It was Sir Greasy Spoon…

They met inside *"Pour La Cuisine,"*
A shop just south of Harlech,
Where Gastro-Pub had armed himself
With bain-marie and garlic,
While England's Pride had donned a helm –
The best to cut the mustard –
Of armour-plated suet crust
And cloak of luke-warm custard…

Sir Greasy Spoon escaped with wounds
Inflicted by aioli.
But Gastro-Pub The Ghastly died
Pierced through by roly-poly.
And, ever since, across our land
Proud folk delight to say
How Gastro-Pub The Ghastly met
His early-closing day.

Sharps The Word For Toffee

It is little I repair to the sweet-shops of the modern folk
Though my inclinations there may blow.
It is little I repair to the sweet-shops of the modern folk
Since they lack the unwrapped toffee blocks by Sharps which used
    to show
Just how dentistry for first teeth could reach sweetly painful heights.
Now what I see are user-friendly, neatly packaged flights
Of regimented wrappers holding pre-ordained-size bites
As my childhood memories flicker to and fro,
To and fro:
O my hammered shards of stickjaw long ago.

Now I peer through sweet-shop windows with a sense of sharp
    dismay
At the lack of dental challenge in the products on display.
And I stand there salivating for a too-long-bygone day
As my childhood memories flicker to and fro,
To and fro:
O my "*Sharps The Word For Toffee*" long ago.

For Tapioca, England And Saint George

Let limp-heart liberals have no doubts;
those days before all kids were louts,
when Englishness held firm beneath
stiff upper lips and gritted teeth;
when citizens slept safe in bed
and half the globe was coloured red
were days when juvenile aberrants
were kept in line by such deterrents
as caning with a kitchen poker
or Nannies' threats of tapioca.

Since caning's banned, I plan to broker
a plan to bring back tapioca
to prompt the glorious re-creation
of England as the world's top nation.

Keeping Up Appearances

Top up my spray tan, Darren,
then phone up *Hello* and *OK*
and gold-plate the taps in the toilet.
The Beckhams are coming to stay!

I've just origamied the Andrex.
Have I time for another tattoo
in spurious Chinese, with dragons,
or maybe a tasteful *Stuff You*?

My wife's nails are covered in glitter
and her eyelids and midriff as well.
Her extensions are tearing the roots of her hair
which is rigid and reeking with gel.

But she says that it's hard to look "current"
when Manolos are something she lacks
and her nipple ring's only nine carat
and it's days since she last had a wax.

Time, Ladies, Please!

Much have I travelled past the late-night bars
and many drunken youngsters have I seen
whose vodka shots and alcopops have been
thrown up into the streets or over cars
by girls in belt-width skirts and skimpy bras
with nothing but goose pimples in between,
called Kayleigh, Karly, Kylie or Charlene,
too drunk to stand beneath dawn's fading stars.
And then I wonder what can be the gain,
except to satisfy the taxman's yen
to make his tithe more easy to obtain
from scarce-pubescent girls and not-yet men
by granting longer hours for each Charmaine
to throw up nightly on some prick called Darren.

Sunset On Empire

Whatever the weather, at all State events
we waited in thousands, excitement intense,
for the chance of a glimpse of a well-practised smile
affixed to the Monarch for mile after mile,
for the clatter of horses, the thrill of the band,
a vestigial wave from a royal white-gloved hand.
And though we were stuck at the back of the crowd
and saw very little we used to be proud
of the stage-managed grandeur and bling by the ton –
Ruritanian pomp in its fast-setting sun –
a reminder of times when our monarchs were head
of a globe mainly coloured a comforting red;
where folk of all creeds and all colours would sing
God Save who we'd told them would now be their King.

Greengrocers' Apostrophe's

Carrot's and Broad Bean's

Why make a fuss?
Soon nobody will care,
not even us.

Or us' !

The Last Post

Once we sent letters on Basildon Bond
To friends and relations of whom we were fond
And with pen and real ink they all used to respond
Via a system as slow as a snail.
Now refinement is gone and we've nothing beyond
Just illiterate texting and email.

Screw the cap on your Quink and your Stephens Blue Black,
For calligraphy's dead and there's no going back.
When the man with the little red van gets the sack
There'll be no more collecting or sending.
And your dog will be left with one less to attack
When the whole postal service is ending.

Calling Doctor Fell

I still don't love you, Dr. Fell.
My reason's not now hard to tell –
You won't come out when I'm unwell.

You claim it's admin overload
That keeps you stuck in office mode.

Appointments offered weeks ahead
Are pointless if by then I'm dead.

Plus, just a bare-five-minute slot
Won't be enough for what I've got.

And once you've found me on your screen
My time is up. That's it. I've been!

It's all too clear I'm seen by you
As health and admin problem too.

You've lost the Hippocratic Touch.
My lack of faith in you is such
I can't think why you're paid so much.

Confiteor Deo Omnipotenti

Before Rome set its adamantine
face against the old Tridentine
all Catholics took the Bread of Heaven
complete with proper Latin leaven
in Missals fat as half a brick,
two thousand pages Rizla-thick
in which it took this boy an age
to ascertain the proper page
for prayers whose arcane rigmarole
they'd said would save his wretched soul.

This Mass which stood tradition's test
is finished. Ite, Missa est.
Salvation now is near at hand
in language we can understand;
and reaching it should be less hard
with Mass pre-printed on one card.
Yet Catholic awe for What Comes Next
seems missing from the English text
and makes this ersatz Mass, for me,
seem precious close to blasphemy.

Maddening Minorities

When our world was much calmer and simpler
and the Media fed us real news
plus humour and crosswords, their mission
it seemed was, "Inform and Amuse."
Now they force-feed us lectures by zealots
convinced that each rabid minority
is entitled to ram its convictions
down the throats of the rational majority.

So the Media's full of the panting
of hectoring luvvies, the dungareed ranting
of crusading wimmin, of Human Rights-Benders,
of P C fanatics with puzzling new genders,
equality-mongers and S. Chakrabarti,
the climate change despots, the rump Lib. Dem. Party...
To Hell with them all. I'm leading the way
for a "Freedom From Maddening Minorities Day."

Sounds Poor, If At All

There's not a play on BBC
with dialogue that's audible,
although I've boosted my TV
with gizmos scarce affordable.

The best directors now, I fear,
the BBC's attracting
claim mumbling adds to atmosphere.
It won't. It's simply lazy acting.

What's more, I'm waiting for the day
the BBC wakes up and drops
its sad misuse of "might" and "may"
and ever-present glottal stops.

I'd gladly pay the licence fee
if it would once more wave the flag
for proper English and RP.
God help me, how I miss John Snagge!

The Bard on Television's Weather Girls

Why didst thou promise such a beauteous day
And make me travel forth without my cloak?
By what right did you give me last night, pray,
A forecast that was such a total joke?
For barely was I one mile down the lane
When Noah's flood descended on my head
And piercing stair-rods of un-forecast rain
Soon turned to marsh the ground where I did tread.
Does Television have no young girl there
Who knows a thing about the weather due
Or has the slightest semblance of a care
For more than preening and an Autocue?
   No man can trust your words when all you seem
   To care about is simpering on my screen.

Spying On Nature

I'm fed up with films which show every last spasm
Of animal courtship, and final orgasm
By shiny-bummed monkeys or whales with a dong
Which is questingly mobile and several feet long,
Or mantises starting their cannibal lunch
Where love, lust and mealtimes all come to a crunch;
Of fish fertilising their eggs in the weed
By "doing an Onan" and scattering seed
While spied on by cameramen for our delight
Then screened in my sitting-room night after night.

Phone hacking is nothing to what we inflict on
The wildlife which TV presenters have picked on,
Spied on, pursued, interrupted and fumbled,
Attenboroughed, Oddied and Packhamed and Humbled –
No dormouse left dormant, no tern left unturned ,
No coitus left private, no chance ever spurned
To show us in close-up on wide HD screen
Their arousal and climax – and all in between.
I speak as I find from my own small experience –
Sex is more fruitful without interference.

Let voyeurs stop filming. Let Peeping Toms cease.
If we want the whole natural world to increase
To the point at which most of it's safe from extinction
Let's draw a firm line and let's make a distinction
'Tween what should be filmed and what quite simply can't
Without making kids snigger or shocking your aunt.
If films are made just for the prurient viewer
Shy animals' matings will only get fewer.
But leave them in peace and there's one thing I'm sure of –
Our wildlife is something there might be much more of.

A Requiem For The Smallest Show On Earth

I weep for him who trained those circus fleas.
For all his livestock, sadly now redundant,
still kept in luxury and well-fed ease,
are every day more pointlessly abundant.
The skill with which they used to strut their stuff
with tightrope, parasol and glitterball
was one which kids once rated high enough,
but on today's scale do not rate at all.

For fickle fashion sings with Siren voice.
Now Alton Towers, frightening and vast,
leaves most thrill-seeking children spoilt for choice.
The day of the performing flea has passed,
its circus vanished and the last crowd gone.
And yet the sound of distant fading cheers
and hopes of one last show still linger on
behind their trainer's curtain-call of tears.

All Together Now

Synchronized nose clips and synchronized Speedos,
Synchronized Swimming's for synchronized weirdos.
synchronized dive-ins with synchronized ripples,
synchronized breast stroke with synchronized nipples.

Synchronized somersaults, synchronized bums,
synchronized studs in their synchronized tums,
synchronized heads up, then synchronized feet,
synchronized pointlessness, synchronized neat.

Synchronized lipstick and synchronized looks,
synchronized codfish on synchronized hooks,
synchronized robots on synchronized swivel,
synchronized silliness, synchronized drivel.

Synchronized wastage of synchronized skill,
synchronized sport rating synchronized nil.
Synchronized watchers all synchronized thinking
that maybe at last they'll see synchronized sinking.

So, Where Now For Jerusalem?

Un-string my Bow of burning gold,
Lay down my Arrows of desire:
Forget my Spear: O clouds unfold
To douse my Chariot of fire!

For I have ceased from Mental fight
And now my Sword sleeps in my hand.
For I'm convinced Jerusalem
Cannot be built in England's land.

About Nearing The Buffers

Inching towards lean and slippered maybe: but with brave flags still flying, loves cherished and a dream still intact.

Time Was . . .

Time was when two and two would come to four –
    never any less or any more.

Then age erased normality, since when
    they've come to anything from one to ten.

Two For The Road

I've reached the stage
when I, too, am relieved

each time my old dog
pauses at a lamp-post.

My wife says one of us
should be put down.

I'm almost sure she means the dog.
But only almost.

Age Has Taught Me . . .

…that the face which views me from the mirror
is no longer mine,

has lost its owner's hair and looks depressed
at what it sees,

…that facial wrinkles are just proof of worry,
not of wisdom

and most things dropped might just as well
stay on the floor . . .

…that tomorrow will seem shorter than today
and only half as long as yesterday.

Thinking Ahead

Now old, we both take furtive heed for one another's future
    and each pretend the other doesn't know

why I have changed your mobile phone for one with larger
buttons,
    fewer functions and a louder ring,
while you have bought an orthopaedic back-rest for my chair
    and moved it closer to the TV screen:

why I have sent away for catalogues of sit-down showers
    and walk-in baths and Saga holidays,
while you have written out a timetable of all my pills
    and taught me how to use the microwave:

why I have added neck-chains to your many spectacles
    and 'lent' your bike to our new Vicar's wife,
while you have added rubber tips to all my walking sticks
    and filled my wine-rack full with bottled water:

why I confirm the route I'm taking when I walk the dog,
    and always try to carry clear ID,
while you have started helping out each weekend at the Hospice
    and now go once a week to Evensong:

why I have checked the value of my life insurance cover
    and you have listed all your favourite hymns.

Mature, gsoh, wltm ...

I'm looking for friendship that might include sex,
Just straightforward pleasure for two. No complex
Or demanding relationship too hard to handle
But enough to at least singe one end of its candle;
Yet one which accepts that an older man's touch
May not move the earth or the heavens too much….

If you'd still like to hope for a strumming of hearts,
For a symphony played on erogenous parts,
For a clashing of planets, a rapture divine,
Shakespearean sonnets and rare vintage wine,
But accept that the outcome, when all's said and done,
Won't be Shakespeare and Chablis but prose and Blue Nun.

And if that is a prospect which might still appeal,
And your hopes and ambitions are not too unreal;
If you're not really seeking a fantasy man;
If your hormones still might and my body still can
And you know perfect love only happens in verse,
I've a gsoh – and you could do much worse.

www.embersrekindled

Internet porn, Internet porn,
nightly delight for the sad and forlorn;
what dreams you revive in my years of senility
now most wishful-thinking outruns my ability
and marital moments of climactic bliss
seldom exceed a demure goodnight kiss.

Internet porn, Internet porn,
with baby oil glistening and body hair shorn
from muscled Adonises filling the screen
with brawn of a kind that my own's never been,
honed pecs, glutes and abs of a perfect congruity,
erections all built to outlast perpetuity.

Internet porn, Internet porn.
The looks of devotional lust that are worn
by women involved in wild, mind-boggling clinches
with male assets measured in multiple inches . . .
With all those exotic positions on show
just where did my faithful old Missionary go?

Internet porn, Internet porn,
melting my pixels from midnight till dawn . . .
Flauntingly, tauntingly, lust now reborn.

No Longer Such A Hardy Perennial

To stop my aged arteries from hardening
I was told to cut down drink and take up gardening.

Some men can take advice, but quite a lot can't.
I compromised.
I gave up drinking tea and bought a pot-plant.

So now if I snuff it during alcohol and sex
I can blame the lack of caffeine – and Begonia Rex.

Fan Mail

Elderly lady, writing from Cambridgeshire,
Violet ink on the edge of the Fen,
Nine O'clock News, plump the cushions, then Horlicks,
Teeth in a glass and your light out by ten.

You wrote me a letter, my very first fan mail.
You asked if I'd published anything more.
And then came another, all green ink and grammar
Which asked me the same thing – and came from next
door.

Elderly ladies, writing from Cambridgeshire,
Lonely and literate down by the Fen,
Dreaming of romance with much-published poets.
I might yet become one, but wish I knew when.

One of you asked me to tea, one to supper;
Scones with Earl Grey, then ham salad and wine
Squeezed from your pensions and Heating Allowance,
Hear your best poems and read some of mine.

Elderly ladies, lonely in Cambridgeshire,
Remembering love on the edge of the Fen,
Competing together in Dunliving House
For moments of friendship in Flats 8 and 10.

At Outpatients With John Keats

When I have fears that I may cease to be
Before the NHS has found the cause
Of why I wake each night at ten to three
And stand before the porcelain while pause
Extends from short to tiresome long delay,
I ought to take much comfort from the thought
My name is first upon their List today
For scan and proctological report.

To "scan" add "probe" the smiling Nurse has said,
Then shown me to a bed behind a screen.
Can hopes of eight hours sleep be worth the dread
Of questing rubber glove and Vaseline?
    Too late to leave! I lie, exposed, and blink
    While self-respect to nothingness doth shrink.

Endoscopy

Please, kindly light,
        amid the encircling gloom
probe gently on.

Searching for any
        last faint trace of Doom
go bently on.

And when you exit
        once more into day
Please God you'll say
        All signs have gone.

Lottery Win

It seems that I've been only slightly ill
despite the blood, the ambulance and pain
as anxious experts poked and probed until
they'd excavated some faint trace of vein.

So put my funeral and wake on hold.
Postpone the lilies and Psalm 23.
This time I've dodged the Reaper's blade. I'm told
I'm well enough to go home after tea.

Once more I've hit the jackpot in health's lottery.
But, in this Ward filled with the sick and old,
I've sensed the staff's well-practised jollity
and seen what next week's losing balls might hold.

Happy In My Own Skin

No matter what state it is in
after years of indulgence and sin,
though wrinkled and sagging from excess of lagging,
I'm happy at last in my skin.

Of regrets now I have almost none.
It's a time to relax and have fun,
since I learned in my youth that the Struggle for
Truth
I'd been fighting for cannot be won.

I'm at ease with new freedom from lust
for each trimly toned waistline and bust.
And I'm long-since resigned every time that I find
that it won't and I can't – even just!

So I've really no cause to complain,
as my time dribbles on down life's drain,
Although, for this liar, the thought of Hellfire
still nags at me now and again.

Though I doubt if there's anything out there
once our toes have turned up and we've died;
no Friends Reunited, no laughter
and probably no "other side."

But I know that you'll wonder about me
as you bid me your final "So long."
So, please, as you do, cross your fingers
and just hope to God I was wrong.

At the Crem

Old friends I see at funerals
now look so old.
    I don't.

Each looks as though the next will be
their own, and soon.
    Mine won't.

Though every time we gather here
they've aged ten years.
    I've not.

Their wives have put on twenty years
and dyed their roots.
    Mine's not.

They moan and whinge that getting old
is totally
    a bugger.

I say I hope we'll meet again,
then go home smug –
    or even smugger.

Old School Hero

Jonathan Bligh, Jonathan Bligh
passing exams without seeming to try;
Head of the School and games-player supreme;
the icing on top of the cream of the cream;
A crutch for the weak and a check to the strong;
protector of those who seemed not to belong;
the apple of many a father's green eye
whose sperm had produced less spectacular fry.
Crafted, it seemed, by some Heavenly whim,
the sun in the sky shone more brightly on him
the *New Improved Version* of Mankind's design,
enough to make Mankind's designer resign –
and God-like enough to be rumoured by some
to have gold thread for hair and no hole in his bum.

Dead! But before the Crem closes the curtain
we're lifting his coffin lid just to make certain.

Mrs. Moseley Leaves Home

A shard of moonlight through the curtains
lights the face upon the bed;
cold and greying, blankly staring
Mrs. Moseley, newly dead.

Down below, with Mother's sherry,
daughters pick at her remains.
Whose the teapot? Whose the teaspoons?
Someone loses, someone gains.

Spoons all counted. Spoils divided.
One decision unmade yet.
Once the Undertaker's finished
who'll take Fido to the Vet?

The shard of moonlight slanting wider
lights the pills beside the bed,
the means, she'd hoped, of resurrection
for Mrs. Moseley, lately dead.

Down the stairs, across the hallway,
latch released with silent hand
Mrs. Moseley, quietly thankful,
off towards her Promised Land.

Drifting rain in Myrtle Crescent.
Daughter lowering a blind
sees a shadow turn the corner,
Fido following behind.

Deckchairs At Eastbourne

When he was tall and she was slim
he fell for her, she fell for him.

And now they're huddled side by side
he is stooped and she is wide;
while dreams that long ago expired
have left them calmer, wiser, tired,
content to watch the sea come in,
go out and then come in again.

But still for her and still for him
he is tall and she is slim.

Finale For Cat And Owl

At an Old Folks Home near a moonlit beach
where once the Bong-Tree grew
live the faded Cast from a tale long past
of a pea-green boat's ex-crew.

Now Puss and her Owl and the ring-nosed pig
and the turkey who'd lived on the hill
slump, mute, in the gloom of a damp Day Room
all wizened and vacant and still

as they wait for the high-spot of their lives
when, every day about noon,
they are fed on mince and mashed up quince
by a Nurse with a runcible spoon.

And as I sang their song to them
I could see that none of them knew
it recalled a scene from how they'd been
in the days when the Bong-Tree grew.

English Soul Food

Aston Villa, apple pie,
Beer in pints, the W I.,

Cricket, Crimmond, bonfire smells,
"Disgusted", still of Tunbridge Wells:

Elgar, Evensong, King Lear,
Fish and chips and Blackpool Pier,

Derby Day, the Boat Race too,
The Hay Wain, Albert Hall and Pooh:

Inglenooks, Joan Hunter – Dunn,
Jerusalem, the Sally Lunn,

King's College Carols, Keats, Bird's Custard,
Lord's, Black Cabs, real English mustard:

Marmite, Beachy Head, mince pies,
Freckled girls with laughing eyes,

Old Moore, The Times, Church fetes, Cream teas...
Please, let me not forget all these.

Last Request

Burn the coffin
you send me off in

and put my ash
out with the trash.

But for better or worse
keep my verse.

Don't bin it.
I'm in it.

Still Dreaming The Dream

No matter how much you cajole it or wheedle
a camel won't fit through the eye of a needle.
You may meet a camel which might have begun to,
but never a needle it's really been done to.
No matter that God once suggested it might
a camel's too large and a needle's too tight.

But if in the sands of some deep desert wadi
you chance on a camel contorting its body
by tucking its hump in and folding its legs,
you can be just as certain as eggs will be eggs
that it's having one last and uncomfortable try
to squeeze through that needle's impassible eye.

And if you look closely perhaps you will see
that the camel still dreaming the dream looks like me.